embryoyo

embryoyo

BY

DEAN YOUNG

BELIEVER BOOKS

a tiny division of

BELIEVER BOOKS

a tiny division of

MCSWEENEY'S
which is also tiny

849 Valencia Street
San Francisco, CA 94110

Cover illustrations by Ernst Haeckel and Sammy Harkham.

http://books.believermag.com

Printed in Canada by Westcan Printing Group.

ISBN 10: 1-932416-69-2
ISBN 13: 978-1-932416-69-5

ALSO BY THE AUTHOR

Design with X (1988)
Beloved Infidel (1992)
Strike Anywhere (1995)
First Course in Turbulence (1999)
Skid (2002)
Ready-Made Bouquet (2005)
Elegy on Toy Piano (2005)

for Jim Galvin
&
Neal Nixon

Let us leave the obedience school.
—John Ashbery

CONTENTS

ONE

THREE

one

Luciferin

"They won't attack us here in the Indian graveyard."
I love that moment. And I love the moment
when I climb into your warm you-smelling
bed-dent after you've risen. And sunflowers,
once a whole field and I almost crashed,
the next year all pumpkins! Crop rotation,
I love you. Dividing words between syl-
lables! Dachshunds! What am I but the inter-
section of these loves? I spend 35 dollars on a CD
of some guy with 15 different guitars in his shack
with lots of tape delays and loops, a good buy!
Mexican animal crackers! But only to be identified
by what you love is a malformation just as
embryonic chickens grow very strange in zero
gravity. I hate those experiments on animals,
varnished bats, blinded rabbits, cows
with windows in their flanks but obviously
I'm fascinated. Perhaps it was my early exposure
to Frankenstein. I love Frankenstein! Arrgh,
he replies to everything, fire particularly
sets him off, something the villagers quickly
pick up. Fucking villagers. All their shouting's
making conversation impossible and now
there's grit in my lettuce which I hate
but kinda like in clams as one bespeaks
poor hygiene and the other the sea.
I hate what we're doing to the sea,
dragging huge chains across the bottom,
bleaching reefs. Either you're a rubber/
gasoline salesman or, like me, you'd like
to duct-tape the vice president's mouth
to the exhaust pipe of an SUV and I hate
feeling like that. I would rather concentrate

on the rapidity of your ideograms, how
only a biochemical or two keeps me
from becoming the world's biggest lightning bug.

Dear Reader,

My nightmares are your confetti
so you may step over tiny skulls
like a satrap among un-housebroken whippets.

The sour diapers of morning
give way to the overripe plums of noon
give way to the designer cheeses of evening.

Then night is no one's problem,
how tender it is with its murderers,
how consoling to its trillionaires,

that lost spaceman music in the pines,
god opening his box of fishhooks.

Dear Reader, I thought
I was prepared but I'm never
prepared but please, take this,

it is your lift ticket, your perfume
that lingers in the fire-fickled room
long after you've vamoosed

and made that poor boy nursing
his third cinnamon daiquiri
realize he missed his chance,

your bones already asterisks,
your chipmunk glance a schwa.

Deadline

Swimming pool full of brown leaves.
The jury files back into the courtroom.
The burning fuse wiggles like a mouse's tail.
Cymbals. Tadpoles. The bearded gods
who battled dragons with big hammers.
Arriving at the café, men with hatchets
in brown shirts. It is the time of fascism
then strangers kissing in the streets
and the time of fascism is over. For now.
The calm of the sea then an armada.
Certainly the meteor is on a deadline,
soon to begin a more sedentary life.
Oh those wild years on a deadline,
the morning full of headache looking
in a mirror that looks into a mirror
where infinitely repeated is an apple tree
on a deadline, its fruit must be finished
by first frost, its buds not open before
the last. Hamlet on a deadline but
not sure which or where. Athens
on a Sparta deadline, swimming suit
an overcoat. Hurry calls one son
to the other across the country.
Running through the airport, running
even on the motorized walkways,
it's best not to carry much.
A great doubt then a great hope
then a certainty. Cymbals.
The longest day of the year,
sunset peacock flash. Ash.
In its DNA, each cell is on a curfew,
lights out, on tables the chairs
turned upside down. I missed my chance

with her thinks the boy hoping not
but being right. Never again
to be alone with her on the porch
cricket cricket cricket
while her boyfriend misbehaves
and a vengeful need ripens in her
as does a third watermelon daiquiri.
The ice melts in the glass, clinking.
The puppy is gone and in its place a dog
then the dog is gone. Friendship
on a deadline, suntans, milk.
The daughter helps her mother up the stairs.
You thought you'd never heal
but you almost did.
The little cart creaks down the street
pulled by a man talking to himself.

Paradise Poem

I swear I'll never drink tequila
until I can fly again.
Problems with the landing gear.
The only smart thing I did
was fill my mouth with crickets
so Duke Sapp could take a picture
of them boomeranging out
but our genius ended there
and he botched the developing
so it was just one blur in another
same as now.
From the practical point of view,
the law of conservation of matter is a joke.
People, prepare for your doom.
We need to get deeper in Dante,
at least to the eagle made of faces
but I'm not ready for the paradise conjecture.
Too much doesn't fit.
Too much of Western civilization is architecture,
bilge, frass,
certain notes only possible
through inhuman squeezing.
I want a phone that rings with a wolf howl.
I want to avoid classical music
bragging about its intelligence,
punk's redundant suicides.
I want to get as close as possible to rain
without actually being in it,
my umbrella in total collapse,
just another metaphysical argument.
I would rather spend an hour with a dying squirrel
than tour a cathedral
although I like the poor lighting,

the tortured frescos
as if you could be threatened into paradise.
I'd miss my bicycle.
I tried painting it so ugly no one would steal it.
I'd miss taking out the garbage.
Does anyone take out the garbage in paradise?
Scrunching the lid down satisfaction.
Dragging the drum to the curb catharsis.
No one in paradise hears the truck at dawn
and thinks it's grinding up body parts.
A rubber doggie squeak-toy
is probably a demonic force. .
A ham sandwich in a paper bag.
I have a slight surprise for you, she said.
What was this angel doing with me?
Wow, a huge scar down the center of her chest!

Pweth

For a while I thought it might be pwelth,
rhymes with wealth. But no, pweth, with
breath. Accidentally, I wrote my Ph.D. thesis
on the hypno-glyph of the teleutonic pweth
but a spot of white paint dropped from a brush
had more pweth. Through extreme concentration
which is the absence of concentration,
I've been able to stop the pweth,
to hold it like a snow globe in my hands.
Trick is not to shake.
I always shake, and rattle, I'm cold, in hurrious need,
don't you hear time's finked imbroglio in the weeds?
Ornery fritillary. Carefully,
I try not to throw myself out the window
to land epistemologically in the Lacanian phlox.
Eric Satie's birthday comes and goes
and barely a notice on public radio.
Artificially, the sonnets of Shakespeare
flavor today's soap operas. Pweth,
more pweth, another wiggle room in hotel havoc.
In poker, the Lord holds all the aces
yet He bluffs. You want proof?
Go to the liquor store. Here's a picture
of the tent beneath the particle collector
where the young physicist waits for part of this
to become part of that. One lesson is the smaller
the calibrations, the bigger things get.
Hours in front of the mirror, still the mirror forgets.
Hours in front of the mirror, now you're all reflection.
Pweth. A single elixir befuddles the knight.
Inexpertly, the hurricane approacheth
the used car lot. Doth pweth originate within
to dart about the world like a dry cleaner's bag

and snag in a peach tree
or is it an imminence of the world,
a doorbell that rings whoever presses it,
or is it what's behind the world
making funny faces? By the end
of the reception, the bride's dress
looks like flypaper. Apocalyptically,
the stuffed bunny lies on the fainting couch.
How I loved looking for the pweth
through Science Hall, past the jars of creatures
who drowned themselves in yellow fluid
just to find out their names
then out the back, past the bent, gristled
pipes that looked much happier in the freezing rain
then through the Iliadic doors
of the Humanities Building like passing backwards
from the Age of Reason to the Age of Sweaty Dreams.
Antiquity had wrecked me,
I always felt snuck up on
like a bird in an aquarium, the message's
necessity always equaled by the likelihood
of its being misunderstood.
Now everyone I talk to
is in a different time zone.
What do you see out your window? I call.
Night, you idiot, they hang up.
But what is darkness compared to staggering with pweth?
Calm? I am calm.

The Saddest Song I Know

Just one variable then poof! everything's
a variable and you're a grown, past grown
shrinking man lucky if your hat fits
a single zip code then suddenly Bing
's singing I'm dreaming yadda yadda,
his croon the distillate of crash and
swoon in a wounded age of sacrifice
and doom, corny sure, behind him god-
fearing violins laying it on thick
and then he's whistling! Imagine,
the Nazis marching through Paris
and you're making a small vault
of your mouth, puckering, and out
comes bird-trill. Probably they're all dead
by now, everyone involved, even the guys
behind the glass in preposterous headphones
who smoke a pack and a half a day, who
knew they were catching something salable
and true and later tried to feel up
a back-up singer in the cloakroom.
Zoom goes by a life, lopsided heart
wild in its tub as the narcotic-alluding
snow zigzags to the ground. Christmas tree
speeding by. Spring drizzle, the bridge
down to one lane for a year, adding an hour
to the commute. Zipping by. The summer
in a leg cast watching friends waterski.
Scalding kiss, the planet like a top,
lofty, furious. Everyone in denim then
everyone in dark suits. Cartoon mice
parading, pipes and tambourines. The girl
stoops to pick up a dime and is 49
by the time she straightens up.

The immortals torn from the groves
like cancelled stamps from envelopes,
the message carried no longer known,
how she wept reading it then went back
to unstitching a dress to make baby clothes.
Body carried through opaline deserts,
glacial cities, through ramparts of cloud.
Meek creatures at the corpses, meek creatures
with huge nocturnal eyes, winged seeds
drawing their equations in the air.
When she left, you thought you'd never
feel again, living above the tanning booths.
Everyone singing gotta gotta gotta then
uh huh oh no no no. Glider thrown
from the balcony, loop de loop
then snagged in a bush scattering
a puff of whistling wrens.

Continuing Instruction

It is not that I love ottava rima less
now that I know it is a verse form
and not a Renaissance hooker. Neither
do I suffer a diminuendo of feeling
for the castle once I've paid the entrance fee
and seen the lousy toilets. No more
the syphilitic viscount shouting for his carriage
long after it's been sold off. His courtesans
too are dust and I do not love dust
less for it. Much needs to be maintained
at greater and greater (impossible) expense
so some is let to slip, that fire escape
looks dangerous, this unfamous tapestry
with its duck-looking unicorn is now
bug-grub, here's some undistinguished weeds.
Disrepair, I salute you, you let
the inside rain come out, the soil gets
enriched, without you there would be no
sublime and therefore, okay, I'm stretching,
no Werewolf Meets Frankenstein or manned space flight.
When your fuel is nearly gone, your weight
is less so easier it is to go further quick
yet that is when you must turn back
if back you ever wish to get. Back
to running shoe lunch meat broken bulb mud.
The headachey travel agent. Stalled
muffin truck in the passing lane.
In the neglected garden, a stone boy
stands beside a living girl, completely
out of sync they are but still attached
the way a word may be to the sky, the sacred

to a mouse. No one knows how sad I am
goes the old song accompanied on thumb piano
loaned, the legend goes, by a laughing wolf-god.

Bunny Tract

Primarily by zigzags like a poem,
bunny moves. Out of base material,
grass is arranged. Certainly, bunny
has much figured out. Quickly, it converts
fear of death, starvation, boredom
into giddy-up, part Chinese checker,
part quantum which is here or there
but never in between. Cherished
by Plains Indians was bunny's power
to disappear by holding very still.
The ancient poet wakes, a bit hungover,
footprints of his friend in new snow
going down the hill, bunny dances
on the edge of the abyss. A cactus
has less in common with static
than a thistle with a kestrel. Baseball
is full of superstition because
it's surrounded by infinity, played
on a diamond formed by multiples of three.
Full of funny hops, bunny twitches,
procreates, kept alive by a curious,
somewhat gross digestive practice
and, perhaps in recompense, excessive
cuteness except for cousin jackrabbit
who looks like those late photos
of Artaud. To give a jackrabbit shock
therapy would be redundant though.
Bunny glimpsed by headlight: sailor's
delight; bunny in the morning red:
might as well stay in bed. Bunny
munches its radish leaves without irony.
Without irony, bunny dashes down the hole.
A sense of incongruity, feigned ignorance,

or the doubleness of being one place
but feeling you are another is solely
a human blessing/curse, an aid perhaps
in traffic jams but much worse trying
to embrace a lover and feeling stuck again
in the third-grade cloakroom, whiffs of glue.
It is times like these it seems bunny
knows exactly what to do, flee then stop
and disappear but friend, our work is dark
in a darker world of not leaping in the sun
much. Nerves live in the wormwood.
Every canoe is a sad canoe. Bunny
hops in the vetch but whatever holds us
in its mouth hasn't decided yet to bite
or drop us in a fluffier nest.

Levels of Formality

Friend's ex-girlfriend.
It didn't end well but not all badly either.
The stars and planets rush about the ether.
A power outage interrupts the symphony,
the machines wag furiously and choke.
Snap, the dancer's role as anti-
gravitational swan is forever finished.
A match's life: all anticipation then skritch!
three seconds of realization.
How to greet and say goodbye fast enough
to the friend's ex-girlfriend, light bends
as it nears the black hole, the reverse
transcriptase takes its toll. Maybe
the Japanese can help us with their grammars.
A twice-met person in the vet's office
picking up the ashes of her schnauzer—
there's a verb tense! Ex-son-in-law
as your waiter—verb tense! It makes sense
that for centuries everyone in Japan
wrote poetry, an art of all hello-goodbye,
it does not seek to rectify the world
so much as greet a piece of it: squirrel
asleep in petals, bug traipsing across
horseshit, and therefore bid farewell.
Some lived in paper houses,
some galloped about on armored horses,
loyal to a lord and when things went poorly
for the lord, killed themselves. Certainly
that must have kept them un-bored!
It took the French to make boredom into art
and poetry without beginning or end
just as they are able to whip formidable fluff
from egg white which is almost nothing.

Mallarme... his poems seem not so much written
as evaporated. But back to the Japanese.
There is still something of the samurai
about the businessman who has been charged
to bid a zillion yen on a painting
auctioned at Christie's in New York.
What would van Gogh think who made this field
as crazy, miserable, glorious as himself,
colors in battle like a brushfire
with the brush. Soon the painting
will hang in a CEO's office, mostly ignored
except by one member of the janitorial staff.
Un-vast and nagging are such chances.
So late one night, the big boss returns
to find a young man with a broom
frozen before it and goes carefully
to his side where a verb tense waits.

An Excitement of Windows

It's fun to break stuff.
I broke a Plymouth once although
that was not as satisfying
as breaking a refrigerator shelf
which set off a cataclysm
then a profound stillness
whereas the car produced a raspy
whirl then a leaky resignation.
The stillness after something breaks,
after it falls to fortress pieces,
spills its metropolitan innards,
knocks over other things which may then
get in their own breaking mood, perhaps
burning an acre or two, may be
the empirical correspondent
to the realization and acceptance
of death. Just once,
I'd like to take a hammer to a diamond
and see. Ka-ching, wine glass hits
the stone, advantageously,
in regards to metaphor formation,
full of red wine.
Plink, the little thingie snaps off
incapacitating the nuclear power plant.
Friendship broken like a paper clip
bent back and forth: expectation, dis-
appointment, expectation, disappointment.
An attractive aspect of human composting
is after the body's frozen in liquid nitrogen,
it's shattered with a suprasonic beam
into pieces small enough for worms to break
and a tree on top each year repeats
mythologically your death

by losing its leaves,
a kind of breakdown for the tree.
There must be a point where a broken thing
can be broken no more.
Probably, we need protection from each other.
In the distance, a cloud of dust.

Chateau Idiotique

You'd think my brain would be edible
but it's just seaweed tangled in a TV
and my dreams remain attached to me
by silver thumbtacks left over from

the Big Flash that I've traced back
to the first 0.0008^{th} second when
everything was so crammed together,
the angels could hardly lift their flutes.

Later my father somehow managed to dance
with the glass column of my mother
and all the toilets of the Louvre
flushed at once. Before weaving can

commence, a variety of preparatory
operations, involving hexed machinery,
must dash a headline across the forehead
that one will labor a lifetime to read,

god being in one of his Socratic moods,
answering with a question whatever's
asked which is how he giveth me the idea
for the answering machine which should have

made me rich but I traded the patent
for a line of snow, a wisteria that won't
come when called and $200 for passing Go
in a game the Theory Group says makes identity

a running shoe. When you split their skulls,
you find their brains have nearly doubled in size
but crack their chests, you'll find whatever
lived there pupated and left behind alphabetic

dust. But I'm tragic in the good ole way,
have about as severe a paper cut as you can get
from a buttery syntax of bafflement. Say that
a couple times with your big yap shut

then tell me you don't see the signatures
of chaos in your wheat germ and dot-com.
See if you don't lurch about like a compass
aroused by a carousel.

Bronzed

That dusty bubble gum, once ubiquitous as starlings,
is no more, my love. Whistling dinosaurs now populate
only animation studios, the furious actions of angels
causing their breasts to flop out in mannerist
frescos flake away as sleet holds us in its teeth.
And the bus station's old urinals go under
the grindstone and the youthful spelunkers
graduate into the wrinkle-causing sun. The sea
seemingly a constant to the naked eye is one
long goodbye, perpetually the tide recedes,
beaches dotted with debris. Unto each is given
a finite number of addresses, ditties to dart
the heart to its moments of sorrow and swoon.
The sword's hilt glints, the daffodils bow down,
all is temporary as a perfect haircut, a kitten
in the lap, yet sitting here with you, my darling,
waiting for a tuna melt and a side of slaw
seems all eternity I'll ever need
and all eternity needs of me.

Out in the Sapphic Traffic

Aphrodite! You are red wine!
Ha-ha provoking, headache-making!
You are life and swallowing life
while running up some ancient stone steps
and probably almost choking.
I am not as tough-minded as a pope
when I see you in your jog-bra.
Nor do I want to be. Nor did I want to be
who they tied the bib on in the fancy place
but when they brought the bowl
with half a lobster and lots of clams
and must be three pounds of butter in the broth,
I was happy with who I was.
Botticelli too saw the connection
between you and bouillabaisse
which means "boiled to a kiss."
No it doesn't, idiot.
Oh who cares about right or wrong
when Aphrodite flashes her nipples?
Now that I am no longer a hyperbolic youth
able to make love to you 37 times an afternoon,
perhaps my odes are better in recompense.
Here is a semitransparent pebble I picked up
on the way to my EKG.
Probably worthless but it is my heart
so take it. Step inside the lightbulb
of my fermentation, Aphrodite,
and tell me of the heating ducts of your day.
Put your eyelash on my pillow,
I will do whatever you say.

Ephemeroptera

Typically soft bodies, loony legs,
forewings triangular and disco,
sensitivity to Gertrude Stein,
how above the above the underneath.
All the time he's strumming her web,
idling in her alley, the threat
he will be eaten. Uh, uhhhhh.
Lab rats scurry east to west.
A valve is monkeyed with. Outside
his bower he piles anything blue
he can find: berries, beetles,
Bonaparte, swatches of Wyoming sky.
She snorts at his sports car while
he paddles with his mandolin.
Ah love, then his tongue swells up,
he's opalescent snot. They tumble
sometimes thousands of feet, seat
a flotation device. First I see you
at the honey trough then first
I see you on the snow bridge and
it goes on like this, first after first
until my body turns to polleny ash.
They give themselves to the clangor
of the sea, caught in silver nets.
What did we lose when the gods stopped
acting like fools? Not the swannish
aerodynamics or shower of gold coins.
Not the bioluminal boudoir or leaflets
exploding from the lips. She opens
the thesaurus of her legs. He attempts
to grab her neck, armed cousins ten
paces back. To hop on top, buff her
blinker, excite her upside down howling

in the understory but the plot demands
they must be separated. He gets
the poison, she stabs herself.
Miles of blank verse. Protruding
from her elytra, an apology knob.
Pheromone unloosed in his outpost,
bras hanging from a shower rod, a bed
of codicils. Help, help. She devours
his head, isolating the lower ganglion
thereby increasing ejaculation. Star
nursery. Kumquat. He compares her to
a summer's day. An envelope on a tray,
a spray of milt he tries to drag her
through. She begins to dig. A part
breaks off. A whisper reddens.
Sometimes they stay this way for days.

Glider

I was supposed to have died
five years ago so I wouldn't outlive
Apollinaire but they found me
a cardiologist who said Stop
exercising, eat more salt. Now
I've got to watch a thousand more
perked nipples while chewing
my gelato spoon. I've got to tell
the telephone solicitor I don't care
how cheap it is to fly to Disneyworld,
Disneyworld better fly to me.
Only one tuft of snow left
with its snout in the tree crotch
and the world is not gentle with its mice.
In another five paragraphs Apollinaire
will be finished, measles in the lilies,
chorus bashed back and forth like kelp,
that wonky smile collapsed.
Picasso, when he gets the news,
draws his last self-portrait
as close as he'll ever come
to a black rectangle. The merciful
god disguises his way in random
accelerations, nattering pathogens.
A giraffe goes knock-kneed to drink.
Some things can't be bought,
they can only be paid for.
Gussied for a wedding, his mother arrives,
lavish as a flare and lights into
the pretty redhead wife for not
letting him know sooner but no one
knows sooner, no one knows now,
yanking the jewels from her ears and neck,

throwing them in her purse, amplifying
dirt's little ditty until it sounds
like a castle being bulldozed.
And would you sound any different?
Tomorrow: armistice, puppets on crutches
ringing the no-one bell, faces torn
and reglued half upside down. End
of the war Apollinaire loved preparing for,
falling from his horse, saber practice,
detonations like brassieres unsnapped,
the same love poems sent to Madeleine
and Lou, calligrammes on birchbark.
Darling, if you were here, I'd try
to lick your heart. My paces matches
perfectly the litter tugged down
the glutted gutter. In front of all of us:
the grate, the journey under then release
into the minnowy gears of the sea.

Blue Curtain

There is a time for tinsel and it is not now.
Oh well, maybe it is.
Who can know in a world of illusion,
fleshy illusional banquet,
diabolical in detail, baffling
as the feel of felt.
Are they making fruit so large
just to rub it in?
You could wander into a snowy field
and bash two bricks together
and still you're part of the illusion.
Even the guy who took seven years
to eat an entire car, an accomplice.
The instruments that bore into your chest
produce a series of telltale dots,
hundreds of zeros.
Your father with his head slumped to the side—
face in a cloud.
The letter comes and tells you
one way or another—
mist above a river of mist.
The tangerine rind in dishabille.
Yellow sports car.
A song turns into thorns in the tunnel
then is restored.
Close-up of something in the charred bits.
Close-up of the blue curtain,
something behind it leaving.

Resignation Letter

This clam doesn't have the slightest idea
what's about to hit it. Well, maybe
it does but approaches life with bemused
becalmed detachment and therefore death
is no big deal, not to be avoided or bewailed
even by boiling. Wide it slowly opens around
its secret vowel. Doubtlessly there is grace
in resignation as there is a briny sweetness
in this clam. The delivery man rings
a second time then turns away. The bee
bounces twice against the florist's window
then bumbles on. Baby quiets, not getting
what he wants, the rain moves out to sea,
the lava gobbles up the village, villagers
oxcarted to another island sector just as
the old ones did, it's their cosmology.
Past and future seemingly resigned to
simultaneously, the lovers agree to see
no more each other, leaving behind drinks
undrunk and twisted napkins. The student
moves to the next blank leaving the previous
unfilled. So much life we cannot have or
find or repeat yet so much we had and found.
I've made this mistake a hundred times,
one thinks, preparing to make it again.
One day I'll get rid of these expensive
painful shoes but not now, another says,
scanning her closet. Some things must resign
themselves to becoming something else,
champagne flat, the burning log ash,
after the crash the runner walks with a cane
but some must accept they'll never change,
stained tablecloth never unstained,

mark permanent on the heart. You pick up
a clod to throw on the coffin lid but can't
so turn away, dropping it in your pocket.

two

Clam Ode

One attempts to be significant on a grand scale
in the knockdown battle of life
but settles.
It is clammy today, meaning wet and gray,
not having a hard, calciniferous shell.
I love the expression "happy as a clam,"
how it imparts buoyant emotion
to a rather, when you get down to it,
nonexpressive creature. In piles of ice
it awaits its doom pretty much the same
as on the ocean floor it awaits
life's bouquet and banquet and sexual joys.
Some barnacles we know are eggs dropped from outer space
but clams, who has a clue how they reproduce?
By trading clouds?
The Chinese thought them capable of prolonging life
while clams doubtlessly considered
the Chinese the opposite.
I remember the jawbreakers my dad would buy me
on the wharf at Stone Harbor, New Jersey;
every thirty seconds you'd take out
the one in your mouth
to check what color it turned.
What does this have to do with clams?
A feeling.
States of feeling, unlike the states of the upper midwest,
are difficult to name.
That is why music was invented
which caused a whole new slew of feelings
and is why since,
people have had more feelings then they know what to do with
so you can see it sorta backfired
like a fire extinguisher that turns out to be a flamethrower.

They look alike, don't they?
So if you're buying one be sure
you don't get the other,
the boys in the stockroom are stoners
who wear their pants falling down
and deserve their own *Gulliver's Travels* island.
The clam however remains calm.
Green is the color of the kelp it rests on
having a helluva wingding calm.
I am going to kill you in butter and white wine
so forgive me, great clam spirit,
join yourself to me through the emissary
of this al dente fettuccine
so I may be qualmless and happy as you.

Ten Inspirations

1

You decide to make soup.
You do not have any carrots or onion.
Any celery or chicken or leaves.
You have water and salt though.
Boil ten minutes. Serve.
And afterwards this simple soup
may be used to wash your face.

2

You decide to make a masterpiece.
You do not have any paints or thorns,
any genius or paper, any pianos
or sticks or rubber.
You have air though.
No doubt about it,
a masterpiece.

3

You decide to make a god.
Don't have no commandments,
no Renaissance altarpieces, no
relics, tax-sheltered televangelists,
funny hats.
You do have yourself.
Wow, god acts like Walt Whitman.

4

You decide to tell your sweetheart
how much you like humping him or her
but even as you're coming,
his/her nipples stiff as pearls

under your palm, you know
there's something deeper you love.

5
You decide to make a flower.
You don't have any seeds, bees,
bat guano, engravings, pitchforks,
sunshine, scarecrows.
You have a feeling though.
Presto.

6
You decide to make a gift.
You have artificial eyes, education,
lightweight wing material,
electricity, sugar, chlorophyll,
a bedroom, doo-wop.
I can't wait.

7
You decide to make a moon
then realize you don't have room
anywhere to put it.
One moon will have to provide
enough rhyming opportunities.

8
You decide to make a suspension bridge.
You look through a toilet paper tube.
You have the day off.
Call Tony but he's on his way to the Cape.
Watch a TV show about paratrooping supermodels.
Wipe gunk off a surface.
Your cat tells you it's dinnertime
but it's only three o'clock.

9
You decide to make a match.
Don't have any sulfur
or magnesium. No striking surface,
accelerant or slogan. You give up
and sleep and a bride-sized spark plug
tells you to look within.
There's a sea horse.

10
You are in your pajamas
eating cold pizza
when you decide to make a coyote.
Now all you need is a pregnant coyote.

Ode to Hangover

Hangover, you drive me into the yard
to dig holes as a way of working through you
as one might work through a sorry childhood
by riding the forbidden amusement park rides
as a grown-up until puking. Alas, I feel like
something spit out by a duck, a duck
other ducks are ashamed of when I only
tried to protect myself by projecting myself
on hilarity's big screen at the party
when one nitwit reminisced about the 39 cents
a pound chicken of his youth and another said,
Don't go to Italy in June, no one goes in June.
Protect myself from boring advice,
from the boring past and the boring present
at the expense of an un-nauseating future:
now. But look at these newly socketed lilacs!
Without you, Hangover, they would still be
trapped in their buckets and not become
the opposite of vomit just as you, Hangover,
are the opposite of Orgasm. Certainly
you go on too long and in your grip
one thinks, How to have you never again?
whereas Orgasm lasts too short some seconds
and immediately one plots to repeat her.
After her, I could eat a car but here's
a pineapple, clam pizza and Chinese milkshake
yum but Hangover, you make me aspire
to a saltine. Both of you need to lie down,
one with a cool rag across the brow, shutters
drawn, the other in a soft jungle gym, yahoo,
this puzzle has 15 thousand solutions!
Here's one called Rocking Horse
and how about Sunshine in the Monkey Tree.

Chug, chug goes the arriving train,
those on the platform toss their hats and scarves
and cheer, the president comes out of the caboose
to declare, The war is over! Corks popping,
people mashing people, knocking over melon stands,
ripping millennia of bodices. Hangover,
rest now, you'll have lots to do later
inspiring abstemious philosophies and menial tasks
that too contribute to the beauty of this world.

Static City

Some of us sitting around listening to static
and one says, That's nothing compared to the sixties' static.
What are you talking about? says another.
If you want real static you got to go way back,
to Memphis, like when Memphis was still
Egyptian, people still with both eyes
on one side of their nose like flounders
wandering around like wind-up toys
before anyone even knew what static was,
before even the wah-wah pedal as we know it,
bread like 2 cents a loaf, before shag carpet
and modern recording techniques
where you don't like something just flick a number.
What we had back then was crawdad boil.
And rope.
And a couple guys at the crossroads
who sold their souls to a snake,
a fucking snake, man,
because they didn't have nothing else
a snake could use and even if they did.
Absolutely no electric tuning forks,
no designer cowboy shirts,
no atom bombs small enough
to fit in a fucking suitcase, man,
but they had an inkling,
a cerebral spark from knocking their heads
against a wall so long they were getting the idea
that the wall was just an idea, a concept
you could just pass right through
but then there'd be another wall
like when you get through childhood
and there's puberty,
it's walls all the way, man,

but they had this authentic buzz,
a hive in the hedgerows
and when a talking snake offers,
you deal, man, you don't
zigzag prevaricate
because that's the snake's metier,
you just deal even if no one'll ever know your name
except a few devotees,
oddball ex-cons, misfits with no gas money,
maybe only a couple on the planet at any one time
knowing the true static
behind this stepped-on, pooched-out
beep beep thunk thunk fluff
everyone's plugged into now,
propagating like cellophane,
like it's raining diamonds on the wedding parade,
like it's god's first thought
and they were around to hear it
and it didn't grate their brains like cheese
which it would, man,
you'd hit the dirt,
everything ripping up your heart
like a horse that wants to head home
only home's on fire and your mind's the fire
so all you can do is rub dirt into the fire
which is your mind like I said.
And you're telling me you ask
someone like that for identification?
No, man, you just know
or you don't and if you don't
you won't ever. Imagine a frog
in your mouth, struggling.
Now imagine you're that frog.

No Self-Control Ode

When I won't listen to your advice
it's not that I am incapable of hearing
like a deaf ship the foghorn doesn't,
it is control over what I feel I have no
which impedes and unimpedes me,
impulse un-turned-about by gloomy spreadsheet,
speeding towards rocks of now-more-too-muchness,
putting whim into action just as acid
must and yeast although a major portion
of my action resembles inaction,
lying sulking moaning on the couch,
curled into a ball the voyager whimpering
in the stationary station not knowing where
he's going, not even the candy machine working
then pop and up flaring and stirring,
pushing, no more shirking, boxes packed,
forms filled, fiscalization of thirty years,
wiping even the corpuscular under-sink,
sleuthing out the garage stink, poor
critter crumpled dead hiding from the cat.
Cat! To the vet! Dumb hat! To the trash!
Surrogate fatherhood! Uh, what?
Mother to assisted living box.
Full stop. Ichthyous is the night,
oh let it all slip, unbalanced the checkbook,
ungraded the dumb essays, unchained
the melody, I can't go on then go I on
unheeding rumble strip and surgeon,
my own way through the thicket, own ticket
to a toy train punched I've only myself
to blame and avoid.

Ground Frog's Day

We rushed our run with the mules of Pamplona
to catch the return of the swans of Capistrano,
a bit mangy from the flight. Sad what acid rain
had done to the answering machine tapestries

of Turin but the Gardens of Hanging CEOs
of Babylon restored us. It was there I once
asked you to marry me, or someone like you
who wasn't specifically driving me crazy

while the blouse-makers of Kansas City
sang their bawdy idylls, not to be brought low
by mad eggplant disease. Never would mere danger
tape keep us from the prosthesis mines

of Flanders where millipedes discharge
hydrogen cyanide when squeezed. I thought
when a man is in the presence of doubts,
Mysteries, uncertainties, there's nothing

better than the dried-out fountains of Retrograde
where your spit foretells the hour of your doom.
But I was wrong and lost you in the valium fields
of Tibet or was it in the House of Mozart's

aneurysm? Maybe you remember my pledge
on the tilt-a-world of Vatican City
or the pledge of someone like me when
our hair was cut straight across our foreheads.

But I don't care, I'm not coming, I've had
enough. So lay me, my darling, in a field

without history or name that I may sleep
until the quack of dawn.

13 Piercings & Still Not Punctured

Youth, how wonderful to sit with you
in the cafeteria, you make Shiva
look like an amputee. I like this jelly,
I say, how they left in the seeds.
Yeah! You pop, and the fact it's flying
at such high speed! Youth, to be with you
is to drive the interstate without a windshield.
No wonder you can hardly stay in your clothes
and therefore wear almost none. I doubt
it's possible there's a death's head
under all the phosphorescent flesh
glued over an antigravitational fuselage
sponge-side down. Even in the classroom,
you're alpine skiing, spectacular wipeouts
even reading Wordsworth: proof he smoked
dope, plagiarized Tennyson, his dependence
on recollection really on forgetting.
Youth, your brain is more hand grenade
than a sack of scholastic slugs, tattoo
barbed wire circles your bicep, eighth notes
home in on your honeyed crotch, even
your barrette shouts, Get out of my way!
How is it possible for you to fall apart
every hour and still hop up for curtain calls?
Youth, I remember when I was always late
because I had so much time. You were waiting
then you hurried on.

Sneeze Ode

Here comes the sneeze with its end of the world
mobster motor, agog cog.
You better not be holding nuttin full,
better not got hurt ribs.
Rip right through your billet-doux, weed-whip
your honeysuckle before the bees get sip.
Unlike its wussy brother hiccups, its argument
is politics not music, neither poetical like the cough,
if there's blood it's on the walls
not in no hark-a-lark hankie.
Flu's coup but too like the wow in wooing,
there's nothing you can do, not the court
stenographer, not the pilot or his co–
so think about that next time landing in O'Hare.
Even the cathedral's cracked in the lunette,
there's an owl in the icicle, a demon
in the lemon, semen in the seaman
and out out it's got to come.
Opposite of humdrum, nowadays
it's the god's only visitation right,
not a shower of gold but a cold draft,
no whole swan but a feather tickle to the nose
then kerBOOM your body's not your own,
its shrapnel in orbit for years and years
before burning up in the atmosphere.

& They Laide Myne Own Body
Upone th' Wooded Bark
& Set Me Afyre & Set Me Adrift

Fortune approached me with her calculator,
a robust sign of her neediness. I'd been
inhaling erasure fluid as you can't see,
just another ex nihilo yoyo grazing
on the classical radio waves
with a sense of the fragility of all life
and the persistence of styrofoam. Of course
it wasn't fair. Some people born
with long legs, others covered with feathers,
hardly people at all. Since defibrillation,
I'd been superficial but only on the surface,
deep down was an emptiness only the loon's cry
could fill. Few contemporaries could tender
such pathos, most of 'em opinionated bananas
gone spotty, litigious, gonadally overdetermined.
But thank god for Mexican ska! It helps
clarify heartbreak just as a golf course
may clarify being struck by lightning,
my valentine. Fortune, meanwhile,
kept trying to knock an eye out of the sky
with a laser pointer to explain the cutbacks.
I knew her family hailed from the old country
but which one, there were so many, older
and older with osteoporosis of the statuary,
buggy in the checks and balances, getting retrograde
notions whose time had not yet come. Again.
Like how Jesus and Shiva and Bob Marley
were really extraterrestrials, the kind kind
you don't see much anymore, being under
the thought-dominion of evil sacks of slime
as we are wont to elect. Let me tell you,

it's a lot to take in for an addled yolk
from the midwest where just dragging your trash
to the curb's like a whole day's work.
Sorry to ruin your party with this hairball.
Let's just say an air of motorcycle exhaust
propels us to the crack-up of our final reward
where we will be judged by a hyena-headed god,
soaked in the sweetest nectars, stuffed
with oysters, raisins and stale bread
and served.

Foam Ode

My experience with strange suds—
not exactly my first memory
but close, some weird froth
in the gutter, Mommie what is it?
Mother telleth not. A big pipe
goes into the creek and turns it white,
no salamander or crayfish after that.
Some crazy retard trying to sing along,
high tide mark a spumey residue.
Nowadays the stuff's everywhere
because of flushable cat litter
and hog farm runoff where the piggies
are cramped in inhuman conditions.
Some, each because of oil,
containing seems a rainbow.
Frog spawn to industrialist,
in a bubble we all started out
like the world inside its atmosphere
in the bigger belly nothing of outer space
working up to burst and be born.
For his last afternoon, Basquiat
snorted coke and ate caviar
then came from his mouth a wondrous pink foam.
And when I went home I thought alone
there you were standing in my tub
outfitted in only soap suds,
word balloon with nothing in it
but a moany oh.

The New Savagery

What does the new savagery
require of me? If I pound a nail
into the wall, the wall is my heart.
All that gnawing on my own headbone—

that was the old savagery, a lassitudinous
charade, black leather jacket boom boom
long after the sun had set and all
that was left was for the dancers
to put their clothes back on.

The mind twists its silver wire.
A tiny mechanical bird is made to sing.

I will write another long last letter
about what I had for lunch, what had me
and you will understand my feelings,
how they only want to feel yours

and if the duty of my dejections
takes me into the sky, no one
must follow me. Not mother
made of balsa wood, not father,
the plinth. Even you, my love,
must not get covered with that ash.

Why am I so afraid of nothingness?
My soul is a baby wolf.

No Forgiveness Ode

The husband wants to be taken back
into the family after behaving terribly
but nothing can be taken back,
not the leaves by the trees, the rain
by the clouds. You want to take back
the ugly thing you said but some shrapnel
remains in the wound, some mud.
Night after night Tybalt's stabbed
so the lovers are ground in mechanical
aftermath. Think of the gunk that never
comes off the roasting pan, the goofs
of a diamond cutter. But wasn't it
electricity's blunder into inert clay
that started this whole mess, the I-
echo in the head, a marriage begun
with a fender bender, a sneeze,
a mutation, a raid, an irrevocable
fuckup. So in the meantime: epoxy,
the dog barking at who knows what,
signals mixed like a dumped-out tray
of printer's type. Some piece of you
stays in me and I'll never give it back.
The heart needs its thorns
just as the rose its profligacy.
Just because you've had enough
doesn't mean you wanted too much.

Sean Penn Anti-Ode

Must Sean Penn always look like he's squeezing
the last drops out of a sponge and the sponge
is his face? Even the back of his head grimaces.
Just the pressure in his little finger alone
could kill a gorilla. Remember that kid
whose whole trick was forcing blood into his head
until he looked like the universe's own cherry bomb
just so he'd get the first rip at the piñata?
He's grown up to straighten us out
about weapons of mass destruction
but whatever you do, don't ding his car door with yours.
Don't ask about his girlfriend's cat.
Somewhere a garbage truck beeps backing up
and in these circumstances counts as a triumph of sanity.
Sleet in the face, no toilet paper,
regrets over an argument, not investing wisely,
internment of the crazy mother, mistreatment
of laboratory animals.
Life, boys and girls, is ordinary crap.
Pineapple slices on tutu-wearing toothpicks.
Those puke bags in the seatback you might need.
The second CD only the witlessly bored watch.
Some architectural details about Batman's cape.
Music videos about hairdos, tattoos, implants and bling.
The crew cracking up over some actor's flub.

House of Geodes

It is now clear that eating your own brain
will make you mad. Because of the contaminants.
Because of the mornings you wake up crying
then rearrange your refrigerator.
Too much pineapple.
Because you come to the edge and look into the nitrate.
Because a hand comes forward and strokes your face.
Because a star requires absolute darkness
like a mouth.
Because three lives later, there you are.
The superlative stalks back into the catacomb, mandibles clicking.
Because the messenger has stopped to get drunk.
Because of seeing the sky in the ice.
Hacking at it.
An outbreak of severalness in the asylum of singularity.
You're forgetting your other red glove.
On the inside, the brain is covered with gold foil
to pull in the radio signals
that hurt your fillings.
Now I have some further questions.
Have you ever been stung by a jellyfish?
How did you ruin the birthday party?
Has that high whine persisted?
Were you left behind or accelerated?
What did she say to you when she was done talking
and you bent down toward the cold body?
As much as I love your handwriting
I do not need to see it in the sky.
Someone long ago built a house of geodes,
now it's knocked down.
If you concentrate hard enough,
you can see the forest undulate
like it's about to burn.

It is how matter moves through the world.
The eel is only one form of the basic conjecture.
Every word is from elsewhere
and wants to return.
Because it has taken us so long to understand
our liberty, we are permitted to join the others
pacing the sunny gravel yard.

Glow Ode

My best idea so far had been
to take a girl to a half-built house
and feel her up but bras back then
allowed a woman to feel secure
knowing if she fell from an airplane
into the ocean and was snagged and dragged
through the water by 50 mph barracudas
her foundation would remain in place
so you'd think I'd be better prepared
but some experiences can only be true
if you're not prepared. I love those fools
who think they can sit out the hurricane,
how later they wave from their roofs
with their parakeets at the helicopters.
And people sleeping in public, when
they drool and bob their heads,
a special device projecting their dreams
on the wall, a pretty messed-up show.
I too have been half in love with Easy-Doze.
I have a poster where you look at the trees
and can't see the giraffe. For a while
I was in danger of becoming someone
who gets up in the middle of the night
to make sure the flashlight in the drawer is off
then I found the giraffe! Happiness
is that unaccountable, my buddy
aging backwards when he found
his young squeeze. He's started listening
to music again but I still need to steer him
away from divorced cowboy suicide songs.
And Blake's still a problem.
And I'm still amazed no one noticed
my new floor until I told them,

how it makes the whole kitchen glow
and one of the guys who laid it
only had one arm!

The First Part of the Problem
Usually Contains the Given

The boat finally comes, a kangaroo
or kangaroo-like eidolon at the helm,
okay? If it's radial division,
it's a geometry problem, vertical:
calculus. My head, a conic section,
was conjoined to the inabsolute so
I got into the boat even without
Aphrodite showing me her bosoms.
It was the third year of my four-year contract
so just being in a boat with Aphrodite
felt good like when things are similar to other things
making them less terrible and unrecognizable and time-consuming.
Which is why babies can't talk because
all they'd say is What the FUCK is that!?
I was glad I wasn't a baby
or a porous robot
or part of me wasn't
so I could float if necessary.
We were underway.
What a strange use of under.
Under consideration.
Under construction.
Under a rock.
Under us creatures made entirely of brain
lit into each other
much as in the sky.
Aphrodite was already deep into her novel.
The contessa threw herself from the tower.
I tried to keep my mouth shut
so the bird I was smuggling wouldn't escape.
Reaching into the ice chest
was like reaching into the infinite

but I didn't know where it would all end,
trusting this ghostly kangaroo,
Aphrodite warm and gooey under her nonpareils,
my heart a larkspur at sea.

Coming from, Going to Ode

A whole lifetime in the middle, no wonder
we crave and fear beginnings and ends.
We want to see Highway 80 vanish
into the Pacific waves, Tolstoy as a baby
trying to hold a pencil. And this endless mess
of photos, could that really be grandfather
dressed like a little girl, mother with flowers
in her hair? The body weighed after death,
what's missing? For a price the ashes
can be pressed into a crystal but
go back to the old neighborhood
and everything's been taken apart,
reassembled wrong, smaller trees, higher
fence around the graveyard where on a dare
you searched for a stone with your own name.
Either the universe keeps going or collapses
closed but for his whole life a man
can be 16 or 49 or 55 or 23
yet he knows he's a volcano.
And every day a woman flagging traffic
knows she has only a couple hours in the sky
rivaling the morning star. A melon slips
from the hands and explodes like laughter,
red, sweet, full of dark seeds.
Behind you a whisper, in front a windy blur.
Soon that face just below the water
will be your own.

Pitchblende

All I ever wanted was ecstasy
so I tried to fathom the fluttering
toward me dead things I don't recommend it.
What a strange disease I have that you
could be my cure. A mechanism produces
thorny light, a labyrinth made of overlapping
circles, not the crisscross of raiding crows
over meadows where there are no meadows.
No one can open the big doors alone, not if
you push until your fingers explode, oh
my clover flower. The imagination is gleeful
in its agony, even weeping behind its bush,
double-parked cars like rainbow trout on ice,
a disemboweled umbrella stuffed in the trash,
crumbled like a sketch of a bat by someone
who's never seen a bat. So I sat down
and dialed all your old numbers I don't
recommend it and each that was answered
pulled someone from deep cold water
I don't recommend it angry or numbed
with the bends. No one here by that name
then hanging up before my ingenuine
apology, just once music in the background
spiraling through the torn and borrowed world
so I could almost forget the roaring toward us
ball of flames.

Ghost Ode

Yellow pencils composing odes to birdlife,
mostly wrens. Lighting fixtures lay
their odes at night's feet, greatly undressed.
A new form of heartache enters the world,
the leaves blow east to west.
Flamingo feather no business floating by
calling forth an ode. Chair hung on the wall
singing its silent ode of spiritual preoccupation
common to all things that do not touch the ground
like fish who never carry cash.
Stickiness the ode of gum to the shoe
of the phooey-saying deliveryman.
If only I were so stuck to you.
The details grew around the noun
like grass around a bottle left
by the rained-upon couple who ran
inside to sing Let's make a home, an ode,
some fragments found preserved
in mummified Pottery Barn catalogues.
Some pilots fly upside down, threatening
to crop-dust outer space.
People keep telling me they like my shirt.
The mountain reveals its cracked agate heart
and clouds extoll shininess
above the people's capacity to grieve.
An elegy of motorboats, elegy of dawn.
Out of death life comes, a fawn
browsing the daisies left on a grave,
smoke-scribbled eighth notes in the wind.

Dear Friend

What will be served for our reception
in the devastation? Finger food, of course
and white wine, something printed on the napkins.

We were not children together
but we are now. Every bird knows
only two notes constantly rearranged.

That's called forever so we wear pajamas
to the practice funeral, buckeroos
to the end. We make paper hats
of headlines and float them away.

My home made of smoke,
tiny spider made of punctuation,
my favorite poem is cinder
scratched into a sidewalk.

My friend's becoming the simplest man,
he sees a lesson in everything,
in missing his train,
in his son hollering from the first branch,
Dad, guess where I am.

I was with him for my first magpies,
governmental and acting like hell.
And the new nickel
with Washington hard to recognize.

We'd driven by a Rabbit flattened
by an upset truck, jars of Miracle Whip
broken over the toll road in heavy snow.

We watched an old lady

eat a hot dog in a bun
with a knife and fork.

A few emeralds winged off
a fruit leaf.

What happens when your head splits open
and the bird flies out, its two notes deranged?

You got better, I got better,
wildflowers rimmed the crater,
glitter glitter glitter.

We knew someone whose father died
then we knew ourselves.
Astronomer, gladiator,
thief, a tombstone salesman.

All our vacations went to the sea
that breathed two times a day
without a machine.
We got in trouble with a raft
doing what we promised not to.

Further out to be brought further back.

There's my friend in his squashed hat
trying to determine if a dot
is a living thing and do no harm.

He's having trouble remembering street names
but there's still plenty of Thoreau.

All that a human is made of is gold,
very very little gold.

three

The Plural of Crisis Is

What? I'm having trouble telling them
apart. The Cadillacs half-buried
like arrows in the sand is art?
Sick elephant at the zoo and always
what to do about the global crisis,
those who say they knew are most of it.
Suicidal for sure to go on the way
we do but how to shove it in reverse
without ripping the transmission out?
A hole in the sky getting bigger, more
and more bad guys learning to fly,
reels and reels put in vaults but decaying
anyway. Nothing, nothing left of her face!
A spill of red wine on your memorial
dress, oil leaking into harbors where
critters who seek and eat each other
get blocked and flocked with it. No one's
shocked except the bless them young
even if all they do is pierce themselves,
sing songs I can't tell are sung and not
just beat to death. Some dolphins lost,
likely driven nuts by submarines conducting
sonar experiments to locate submarines
conducting sonar experiments gurgle
gurgle Help! The president swears only when
everyone's in jail will we all be safe.

As One Pluck'd from the World and Whorl'd

I'm waiting for someone who can tell me
what happened since I left, since I
dematerialized. Had my writings been dispersed
or organized by a system I could never know
but was always at work, acute, calculable
as the angles at which light blurts back
from the building where once I glimpsed
a movie star eating some sort of melon,
as close as I'd ever come to celestial swing
like a top wobbling down, rotation decaying
to a drunken lunge. A long time ago
when I had friends crazier than me,
when my little duckie finally slept
with enough of them, I got my ring back,
and being conventionally tanked beneath
my Complete-Works-of-Chekhov mask, tossed it
into the weedpatch behind the power plant
where previous artists had left
their monuments half-struck because
they'd found out about the personal life,
the holy man's penchant for milk boys,
the benefactor's dabbling in the slave trade,
a halo losing its anti-gravitational force
to slip over the head like a noose,
the brain puffed and snorted to a roaring
like a hand held up on fire. You could
gnaw a trapped limb off. You could walk
through walls where there were no walls.
Now it is as if my shadow has its own job
sweeping a thousand steps, one day going up,
the next down, scattering the mangy pigeons,
making my way through the earphoned
pickpockets and stranded tribes compulsively

stroking new tattoos the way an insect
will continuously groom itself even though
its antennae aren't dirty but snapped.
Kiosks stapled with warnings, condemnations
and pleas, the nouns rearranged each dusk.
The other ghosts with their helmets and lasers,
their whips and cell phones and dogskin shields
hanging from the straps of buses huffing by,
the sky fanning its dark tail with a million
eyes. We drop into the world, our vision
blurred with blood, gagging for breath,
a 15-digit serial number welded to our under-
carriage. We're dipped in the river
a mile below where the ashes are let go
then scrubbed and laid in coals
to harden us but that never works.

Mule

Is it the dark nuttiness of life
that makes you feel like you're carrying
an immense bell up a mountain,

birds screaming about the end of the world
and instantaneous start of the next,
haze obscuring the troop movements,

a lonesome task narrated by a robot monkey
from a future of only robot monkeys left?
Why would anyone want a bell up here anyway,

trees tuckered out, permafrost tinged
fungus pink, fire only a hundred degrees,
hardly a fever? You could be a killer

and this your penance, a monk and this
your reward. Maybe you can't be resuscitated
and it's best to shut off the machines,

go check the scarecrow in the far field.
Goodbye old pal, you were my squeaky toy.
Goodbye old pal, sorry about your sister.

What you wouldn't give right now
for a mule to accuse and ask forgiveness,
big mule schnoz prodding you on,

a face so goofy and sad it brings out
all your love for this butchered world
like a splinter.

Don't Need a New One,
Just Fix What You Got

You're not going to like this,
says the mechanic. Fine.
I already don't like people sending me
pictures of their children not because
I don't appreciate wee Marta eating paint chips
or Alexander thrashing his horsie
but how does one dispose of such photos
without weird mojo?
And I don't like that everyone gets a frog
to vivisect when a simulation
accomplishes just as much, frogs,
their plight, being a priority of mine. .
Compared to bleaching the planet,
what's an alternator?
60% believe man's created in God's image
but can't see His face in the mantis,
His heart in the dying squirrel.
The gun lobby got the vote out.
Comparatively, what's a problem with the wiring?
110% said the data was tabulated fairly.
Please don't let me become
one of those who won't touch anything
without gloves because of the contagion
although I feel the attraction.
Don't like paper or plastic.
Don't like people leaving their dogs in hot cars,
don't like the football traffic
or the new parlance of emailing courtiers.
Cram as many notes as you want
into Twinkle Twinkle Little Star,
it's still Twinkle Twinkle Little Star.
Christmas lights left up all year

thus robbed of the emotive force
of their redeployment I do not like.
Can you give me a new soul,
asked a guy on Telegraph Avenue.
Yeah, right, another nutcase
but then he started to cry.
Big sober kid in expensive thug regalia.
What happened to your first one?
Defiled.
Him, I liked.

The Father, Supposedly

You decamped to France when I was born
which is why I did not follow, unable
to move my limbs in any sensible manner.
I had grown from a single cell like a comet
swatted between bickering black holes,
my hair the blond of brittle stars
in the wretched surf, my eyes the green
of forests burned to the ground. Lightning
picked me up and grew bored in a solitary
hour then I wrote thousands of whiny
letters I'm still embarrassed about.
But you had your own aftershocks,
Paris like a giant refrigerator magnet,
people diddling away afternoons as
existentialism sloshed into nausea.
Generally too lazy to kill each other,
they stayed so thin and frangible
by hardly swallowing the buttery
buffoonery for which they're known.
Did you ever learn that lesson?
Underwater screams made long ago
circled in huge schools of exegetical
theories while something rotted in the corner
of my crib, delighting the microscopic
minions of the dark, giving them a Babel.
I tried to sit up straight and form the bubbles
of your name. Inside the brain, the readying
chamber below the amphitheater, crowd noise
swirled above like the wretched surf. I'd
hoped for an isthmus but got an archipelago.
It gives me I suppose a certain outlook
of uncertainty, a fucked-up permission—
all those feathers from my mother's side,

the useless armor from yours and still
I'm falling from an airplane into a blue
irreconcilable axiom. Translation:
I'm starting to fall apart, each of my seeds
a wingnut, my mind a crystal grown in zero
gravity, perfect, unable to hold itself up
under its own weight. Ever the crybaby,
cruel, selfish, I tried to get a shout
out to you that all might be forgiven,
given, given what? You are what you always were,
echo, interference, a shimmer on a TV screen,
blizzard on the sun not some ectoplasmic
late-breaking news. The forms that had you
as the answer I tried to leave blank.
You never came back. Me neither.

Search Party

Some people burst in wielding terminology I could not understand
and forced me to sign their petition
although the name I signed was not my own.
Rocks could have done as good a job.

Earlier I had walked the beach and that seemed a raving success,
I avoided the criminal suds and a few persnickety gulls
and a vast expanse opened up and engulfed me
like a jigsaw puzzle of a billion pieces
of a single eye.
It couldn't be solved, only advocated.

I had a wife once, but she too dissolved
although a sweetness remains, a few sticky patches.
Oh, the past is so finely pixelated then they switch off the lights
and all are left to rummage a sole inner dialogue,

the one propositioned by philosophers of yore
when they first felt the woods may in fact be empty
and so too the sky. Many put down their heavy burdens,
rattling the floorboards as if waking from a dream
and wishing not to. The chickens were loose again.

For a long time I had no place to go
and went there and couldn't tell if I'd arrived.
Busy people with drippy umbrellas, to-do lists,
a limitless wattage stranded in the solar plexus
except for gusts of wild pause, wilder flight.

The nighttime is no time to undertake a search
yet that is when we begin and sometimes
must end, a voice in the thicket, a waving lantern.
Over there.

So over there we go, regretfully, trampling the rue
and saxifrage. Already the reporters
are getting it wrong.

Crash Arrangement

So we go to the waves.
Each comes through its crash
as far as it can
some with shreds of seaweed in their teeth
some just turning a stone
some only foam

they aren't berserk with sorrow
or sleeplessness or body parts
wheels empty of wheels
or weeping in the message light
or alone in the pulped after-warble

they don't have to find someone
to take her cat
or cover her Tuesday class.

Newlyweds

Little hurt bat,
I thought you were a teabag
dunked from your necropolis
into the buzzy forsythia.
Hurdy gurdy, says the world
feeling a wee cranky,
morphology pink as a popped quiz.
It's nice in the yellow cistern though,
nice to be a wingéd micey
crawling along on clawed thumbs.
Grungy dumb chum,
how best to swallow you
to keep you safe?
Little erasure rubbing,
Death thinks of us.
Death likes daisy decals on the going-by.
Buckeroo pj's. Naptime on Neptune.
The people who haven't found out
won't a while longer.
Until we can be sure.
That's thunder not road construction.
Iffy Xray umbra.
When my father died some part of me became a stump.
Now it's the greenest.

Wind Off a River

I love the stampede of broken glass,
there's nothing quieter.
I press a scarlet seed into your palm.
Quiet.
It used to be enough to lie in my cradle
letting the planets burst from my forehead
and god would be on the telephone.
Hardly a scar now.
Motorcycles in the middle of the night
think they're winning the argument
just by putting a big tear in the thesis.
But rage is quiet.
A shadow tied up in viscera is quiet.
Let us be clear about how little time is left,
what the avalanche requires of us.
Being drawn into the mouth of some eight-legged thing is quiet.
The center of the sun is quiet.
The last year of my friends' marriage,
although one of them didn't know it,
they'd get to the restaurant
and both start talking
so you'd have to choose
who to listen to, which quiet,
the one like a bottle of freesias
in an office full of broken chairs
or the one like the wind coming off the river
hard enough to freeze the tears it causes
same as now.
The paws of our great source
touch us in our sleep.

Iodine

I'm sitting with my refraction
in our bar, inexactly, according
to some law in the expiration
of foam in our beer. This is easily

my third heart, its agony a by-product
like diamonds inside coyotes.
My bones are big but my head remains
unlocatable. Simple clutch of daisies?

Scribble with eyes closed? There is flight
in my fortune cookie, and nudity.
The tuckered-out underlings of our lord
throw down their lightning bolts

onto our pillows, in our tub.
Today my shadow's a green branch
through my heart. We don't know
whether to pull it out or let it grow,

let its leaves get covered with soot
then turn gold and attract females
of my species. Maybe it wants to fill
me with fruit, bitterer and bitterer

because there's only one river
where we were born and it stays
strapped to the sky. It hurts
when I walk by the store windows,

unmatched boots walking up a wall,
the grocery with its hanging sausages,
the brain-jumbling laundromat.

And when I try to sing.
Or anyone tries to sing.

Inverness Grey

So what is the cause of death? The inner
flying stops, it's mysterious unless
there's trauma to organs, bark or head.
A brick falls on a caterpillar,
not much mystery there but even unhurt,
thriving things seem pointing to their end
especially if psychology's involved.
Smaller and smaller, the sea bashes everything
until voilà: sand. It is 10:30 then 10:34
then 40 years later. Time passing not the causer
but the caused. Baby now in trouble
with her credit cards, no more can you ask
the friend what you never could. The pier
turns to splinters, gown to dust-rags,
life to not-life. Even though everyone
already knows, is death a secret
that must be told and told? Almost sexual
although so many wires in our minds,
it's easy to cross a few. Bend a paper clip
back and forth, it breaks, the molecules
can only take so much. Ann-Margret
bent back and forth. Scarlet king snake
bent back and forth. Wooden ladder.
Apple tree. Every sunset is a crease,
mother weighing less and less but falling
harder. What is the cause behind the cause
behind the cause? Smaller and smaller,
bodies slamming bodies, bent and bent
until only a few traits remain: color, cry,
residue of dream in the corner of an eye,
kiss on an envelope then the flying flown.
To where? Into solar flares? An angel's hair?
The next one over there who's not yet

an embryo. Or does it just disperse,
a spurt, a spark from the flinty gears?
So the sea bashes and bashes and the planes
take off and land and the fluffy murre chicks
waddle off the cliff.

Mortal Coil

It doesn't hurt when the raven
puts its beak into my chest.
It doesn't hurt that my father
forgets my name which is the same as his.
My berserk cat's quieted, all his toys
safely lost.
A small engine whines higher and higher
taking the hill, the drunks downstairs
laughing and running their disposal,
guests gone.
Thank you it doesn't hurt
to say to no one, the fog
passing its sponge over my face.
White rectangles hover about the room
and I can see in the dark almost
as much as the dark can see in me.
I'm sorriest for the parts the raven
won't carry off lying beside my beloved
growling in her delicious sleep.
Everything is circles in circles.
Wind full of circles,
a meadow made smaller and smaller
to fit in a mind.
I remember vexations of extravagant argument.
I remember throwing a bottle against a wall.
Carrying her name in my mouth across snow,
my head protected by watery ovals,
the little birdman crashing into the sea,
a few dutiful clowns behind plows,
a single silver cloud.
And lots and lots of music.
Leggiaro: nimble and delicate.
Martillato: hammered out.

And at night, trains clattering down by the river
even when there are no trains, no rivers.

Complete Poems

Here's the work of Kenneth Koch.
Even the somewhat melancholy poems
are happy. He must have been absolutely
nuts. No, he wasn't. Nor was he
an aluminum snore like Robert Lowell.
Gladiolas arrived at the door. Yip
yip, said the puppy and Yuff yuff
the puppy grown up. About 12 hours
hardly total I spent with him
before he died, Daddy I almost cry,
Oh get over it, he said the first time
coming down the hall, he was tall
and covered envelopes entirely with the address.
There was no fractioning Kenneth
Koch, no parts, you always got
it all, Terra del Fuego got it all,
off-off-off-Broadway, the cab driver
from the Ivory Coast, hurry, the museum's
about to close and must be hustled through,
whizzing past the urinal, dizzy with dots,
oh great splash the size of a dump truck,
I can barely talk when I'm interviewing,
what's he saying now that the tape's off
about his mother in a white nightgown
and Wallace Stevens? Impossible
to imagine his eating a tofu burger
or waiting very long in a car.
He had a letter from Jean Tinguely on his wall
that Tinguelyesque apart t'would fall.
Even with everything there is a point
at which there is no more.

Leaves in a Drained Swimming Pool

Poetry is an art of beginnings and ends. You want middles, read novels. You want happy endings, read cookbooks. Not closure, word filched from self-help fuzzing the argument. Endsville. Kaput. Form is the shape of the selecting intelligence because time is running out. Form enacts fatality. To pretend otherwise is obfuscation, philosophical hubbub of the worse sort. A lie. We die. We go to art to learn the unlearnable, experience the unexperienceable. Art reports back. Form is the connect, primal haunt, carbon chain end-stopped. You can tell it's late because we prefer the songs of Orpheus after he's torn apart. Pattern as much a deficiency as a realization. No one gets to count forever. Irreverence is irrelevant's revenge. When you slice yourself open, you don't find a construct. Bloom rhyming with doom pretty much took care of Keats. Wire in the monkey's diencephalon prints out a wave most beautiful. Open form prone to mouse-droppings just as closed to suffocation. The river swims in the fish. The giraffe goes knock-kneed to drink. The girl ties back her hair in a universal gesture. Theories about art aren't art any more than a description of an aphid is an aphid. A menu isn't a meal. We're trying to build birds, not birdhouses. Put your trust in the inexhaustible nature of the murmur, Breton said that and know when to shut up, I'm saying that. We're not equations with hats. Nothing appears without an edge. There's nothing worse than a poem that doesn't stop. No one lives in a box. The heart isn't grown on a grid. The ship has sailed and the trail is shiny in the dew. Door slam, howling in the wood, rumble strips before the toll booth. Enter: Fortinbras. Ovipositor. Snow. Bam bam bam, let's get out of here. What I know about form couldn't fill a thimble. What form knows about me will be my end.

Son of Fog

When the fog burns off and the air's pulverized
diamonds and you can see beyond the islands
of forever!—far too dramatic for me. It hurts
something behind my eyes near the sphenoid,
not good. I prefer fog with fog behind it,
uninflammable fog. Then there's no competition
for brightness, no Byron for your Shelley,
no Juno eclipsing your Athena, no big bridge
statement about bringing unity to landmasses.
All the thought balloons are blank. The marching
band can't practice, even a bird's got to get
within five feet before it can start an argument.
Like dead flies on the sill of an abandoned
nursery, we too are seeds in the rattle
of mortality. A foglike baby god
picks it up, shakes it, laughs insanely
then goes back to playing with her feet.
I have felt awful cold and lonely and fog
has been blotting paper to my tears.
My dog is fog and I don't have to scoop
its poop with my hand in a plastic bag.
There are sensations that begin in the world,
the mind responding with ideas but then
those ideas cause other sensations.
What a mess. We stand at the edge
of a drop that doesn't answer back,
fog our only friend although it's hell
on shrimp boats. There, there, says the fog.
Where, where? You can't see a thing.

All That Died in the Cat-Punctured Mouse

was needless to the eternal mouse
who gigantically stands over me
as I drop his used-teabag body into the trash,
even the trash standing over itself
with stink by the end of the week
suggesting a thing of beauty may linger
not eternally in the mind but it's not
beauty's fault, it is the mind's.
The mind is made of milk
and refrigeration has its limits.
So while in Italy, see as many Caravaggios
as you can and I will look here in my bushes
and grocery store. I will go through my closet.
It is shadow that brings forth grace
he would have agreed with Leonardo,
some things are truest only glimpsed
although reflectology can reveal
how a ruffian becomes a cherub,
the eyes that were open half-closed,
a hand now lifted to a cheek.
Still as sugar is the house, distant
stays the sea, the eternal part of my friend
must be needed elsewhere which may account
for my continued grief. Come back
it's silly to plead yet the moon comes back
and it is everything to me, the springtime
crickets, cheesesteaks of Philadelphia,
my brain inside a bell until static overwhelms
the broadcast like a fire alarm a history class
and no one runs or screams,
having been so well drilled.

So the Grasses Grow

I would be sad without potato chips
but much worse if you chopped off my arm.
Being sad is a form of exsanguination
so perhaps to the bottom of sadness I could get
as I bled to death. I do not know.
I do not want to know.
Already you took my turtle
and left me the plastic pond dish
and plastic palm tree
then gave me my first funeral.
We buried a jewelry box.
I don't want a spider quadrupling
in the center of my chest, oh spider of pain.
Here, take my Babe Ruth stamp,
my Day of the Dead skull man
with the elk head on top of his.
I do not own a pair of castanets
but take those too. Perhaps
you could edifyingly divert yourself
with 19th-century Russian novels
where awful things happen even though
people think a lot. A lot. Maybe because?
Check out this book of Gorky drawings
especially page 74 but do not take
Brenda, not even one piece
even though you take her mother
who takes a Brenda-piece along with her,
that, I know, can't be helped.
And do not take my love
while she is at her windsurfing lesson
or anywhere between. You already took
her wallet and charged a houseful of furniture,
terrible ottomans, hideous divans, corpuscular easy chairs

before she even noticed, you are that quick!
But how slow you were with my dad,
tooth by tooth, gasp by gasp,
I could tell he was afraid.
I looked down the road
where someone was buying shoes.
Is it possible to choose a pair
solely by the prints they'll leave
in the dust and snow?
I know you have a job to do,
without you there would be no beauty,
no nitrogen cycle or atmosphere or cantaloupe.
No gleam without a maggot, no cloud
without tears, how it smells like iron
then it rains and rains and rains.

ACKNOWLEDGMENTS

Some of these poems appeared in the following magazines: *American Poetry Review*, *The Believer*, *Conduit*, *Crazyhorse*, *Denver Quarterly*, *Fence*, *Forklift*, *Gettysburg Review*, *Hungry Mind*, *jubilat*, *Michigan Quarterly Review*, *Paris Review*, *Ploughshares*, *Poetry*, *Pool*, *River City*, *Slate*, and *Threepenny Review*. Thank yous to those editors.

Many people made me feel that I wasn't wasting my time writing these poems so I thank some of them here. Andrew Leland, Mary Ruefle, Dobby Gibson, Vendela Vida, Matt Hart, Cole Swenson, Wendy Lesser, Dora Malech, Chris Wiman, Kevin Stein, Clint McCown, Seth Pollins, Michael Collier, Keith Ratzlaff, Matthew Zapruder, Bob Hass, Joe DiPrisco, Ed Ochester, Sarah Manguso, Matthea Harvey, Rob Casper, Nate Hoks, Nikki Flores, Rupert Loydell, Shari DeGraw, Sally Keith, Jim Longenbach, Jan Weissmiller, Reg Gibbons, Ellen Bryant Voigt, Mary Karr, Michael Burkard, John Ashbery, James Tate, Charles Simic, Tomaz Salamun, Ralph Burns, David Wojahn, David Rivard, Mark Levine, Emily Wilson, Donald Revell, Kenneth Koch still

and my brother Tony Hoagland

Dean Young has published seven previous collections of poetry, most recently *Elegy on Toy Piano,* a finalist for the Pulitzer Prize, and *Skid,* a finalist for the Lenore Marshall Prize. He has received fellowships from the Guggenheim Foundation and the National Endowment for the Arts and teaches at the Iowa Writers' Workshop.

MAIL
THIS
PAGE

If you fill out the bottom section of this form, tear out this page, and mail it to the address below, you'll quite suddenly begin to receive the *Believer* magazine in the mail. In addition to publishing poems by Dean Young, Anne Carson, Tony Hoagland, David Berman, and others, each issue of the *Believer* also features terrific essays from writers like Rick Moody, David Mamet, and Richard Powers, along with interviews with the likes of David Foster Wallace, George Saunders, Janet Malcolm, Shirley Hazzard, Ice Cube, and Ashida Kim (who is a ninja). Maureen Howard called the *Believer* "a wealth of intelligence, energy, and wit." Don't miss a single issue!

Please send me one year (10 issues) of the Believer *for just $40! (That's a five-dollar discount only for people who read the promotional copy in books.)*

Name: _____ Street Address: _____

City: _____ State: _____ Zip: _____

Email: _____ Phone: _____

Credit Card #: _____

Expiration Date: _____ (Visa/MC/Discover/AmEx)

Please Make Check or Money Orders out to *The Believer.*

CLIP AND MAIL TO: *The Believer,* 849 Valencia, San Francisco, CA, 94110